FANTASTICAL FOR REAL

PROSE POETRY

ANN GARCIA

RIVER BLOSSOMS PRESS

ISBN 978-1-7372735-0-9 (pb)

ISBN 978-1-7372735-1-6 (eBook)

Cover art by Ann Garcia

Cover design by River Blossoms Press

This chapbook is dedicated to those who believe in my words.

∾

The Composer's Canvas
(from me to you)

Linen fibers thirst, so words will quench their cry, within which lines of soul will spell a truth inside a rhyme. For there is sung a dreamer's song— inked favorite shades of black—conveying soulful memories where fantasies have hatched. These blackbird notes will find their way and nestle here and there, taking flight in poetry my heart, alone, can share high up above in hopeful sky, limitless and blue, where flights of fancy and delights shall carry me to you.

CONTENTS

PREFACE

Dear You,

Welcome to my debut poetry chapbook for which I've selected prose poems inspired by a metaphysical connection between a soul mate and I—a fantastical (for real) experience that resulted in significant inner growth.

The poems presented here weave appreciation for nature into my concept of the creative's self, the creative's soul mate, and the potential found inside where hopes and disappointments play tug-of-war while the soul plans its triumph.

I invite you to escape adulthood, think outside life's box, and join me on a (self) love journey for a few precious moments.

Sincerely yours,
Ann

SELF MEETS SOUL

I caress pages of My Valentine Blue beneath a February moon at midnight.

Alone by the stream where we used to collect summertime pebbles, I pull my coat tighter to preserve remnants of my warmth. Snow is falling on the water, which is losing its battle against the cold. Soon, it will be frozen—its passion will writhe beneath an icy surface, unable to flow freely. Unable to express itself. Just like you, My Valentine Blue.

Too sweet you are.

For them.

Too loving you are.

For them.

Too knowledgeable you are.

For them.

Too passionate you are.

For them.

You are too much you, My Valentine Blue. But I love you true, so I caress you beneath a February moon at midnight.

The chill invades us, telling us we aren't wanted.

We aren't good enough.

We aren't worthy of being seen.

We should be still.

Be silent.

Be nobody.

I caress pages of My Valentine Blue beneath a February moon at midnight.

I'm ready to let us fade into the forever silence of a heart broken by an unrealized dream. My hand places you in the water, but I can't let go even though iciness bites my skin.

Pain of letting go is greater than pain of holding on, so I follow you into the rushing stream and soak myself in the cold until the February moon goes black.

I wake to a voice.

Gentle.

Loving.

Sure.

My Valentine Blue calls me from somewhere warm inside my hope.

A fire burns by my bedside where The Rescuer reads dried pages of my love, My Valentine Blue.

He sees her.

He breathes her.

He believes in her soul.

He loves her just as she is.

Without censure.

Without shame.

Without hiding her name.

Reality shifts into dreams anew as I gaze through my window and find a February moon.

I smile a weak smile as The Rescuer takes my hand and kisses it to remind me that love is our truth.

Ever fierce.

Ever real.

Ever me.

Ever you.

May our future be bright,

My Valentine Blue.

I MET A LOVER IN WORDS—A
DESTINED FRIEND—WHO BOUND
MY WILL TO STARLIGHT TUCKED
INSIDE MY INTUITION.

FOR THE SOUL MATE

I just read the moment I fell in love with you. It was written through quill of ages inside my heartbeats. Destiny placed me inside the girl who picked a flower from a puddle and tucked it inside her deep for you to find, using quill of ages and a lover's mind. Afraid, yet strong. Hesitant, but determined. Unaware of feeling the moment I fell in love. With you, cosmic intention made itself known by giving tears from a sky that fed a love felt everywhere, through everything inside me. Please never let go of your delicate daisy chain.

COSMIC INTENTION, YOU AND I, AS
GIVING AS A TEARFUL SKY ON
MOONFLOWER BLOOMS IN
MEADOWS VAST—OUR PRESENT
TIED TO RIBBONS PAST. WHEN
YOUR EYES CLOSE, I SEE FOR TWO;
INTUITION KNOWS WHERE SKIES
ARE BLUE, SO TAKE MY HAND, MY
DESTINED FRIEND, AND WALK OUR
PATH AS IT RISES AND BENDS.

*T*he special place reserved for you had lain beneath dust thickened by dismissed dreams for uncountable years.

It was our purple palace—the one I dreamed up as a little girl —all cozy beneath my heaven's staircase in a house that didn't exist. It was my refuge. I played there with my twin that, like my peaceful home, didn't exist.

She was my reflection.

My other me.

My playmate when times were quiet, and I was free.

Oh, how I longed to meet her, my other me. Together, we would build castles, dance daydreams, and sing soul songs that nobody would hear unless we wished it. She and I were to be a force of delight. Happy and full in our purple palace, we would be strong, always safe from the world of undeserved spite.

But my other me never came.

This special place reserved for you had lain beneath dust thickened by dismissed dreams for uncountable years.

My other me.

My reflection.

My playmate when times were quiet, and I was free.

Oh, how I longed to meet her. But age would have its way. Wisdom came.

It took uncountable years of dismissed dreams to realize that I should not have been looking for another She.

My twin dreamer, you blew away the dust, awakening dismissed dreams of uncountable years. You'd been waiting in the north tower for celestial ages. In our purple palace. The one we dreamed up as children. Beneath our staircase. In our home that was always there. The one my little girl soul did see.

Because your home was inside me.

I wake with a poem on my tongue and a kiss on my lips.

Beatings of your heart song whisper in my ear as it caresses your chest, bare and brave, in a fair field of daisy chain dreams. Your touch slips inside my awakening, teasing out breaths where the oak sentry stands strong and tall under summer's sun in a cloudless sky.

Years since first flutters of knowing had passed into darkness and doubt and into light again, leading to this moment of calm. This moment of fulfillment. This moment of *we* under Fairytale's canopy.

I wake with a poem on my tongue and a kiss on my lips.

Snuggled deep inside possibilities on dewy blades of morning, I see the universe inside your eyes. It looks into me with reflections of yesterdays and assurance that tomorrows will keep me safe and warm and tucked inside all that is good within ultimate form.

My lips brush your cheek to welcome tears of knowing the same. Your heart song pulses inside my veins as I savor the fantasies you weep. Cry, my love. Cry this moment of fulfillment. This moment of *we* under Fairytale's canopy.

I wake with a poem on my tongue and a kiss on my lips.

Your touch slips inside my awakening, teasing out breaths of us.

Sated, I look up. Beatings of our heart song beg us to dance on the emerald floor shining atop Fairytale's canopy.

I smile at the universe inside your eyes.

I take your hand.

And we *fly*.

I WONDER AS I WANDER 'NEATH A SKY
THAT FEEDS THE STARS. WOULD
YOU FLY ME UP TO HEAVEN OUT OF
REVERENCE FOR MY SOUL? HAVE
US DANCE THE SCALES WITH LIBRA
TILL THE ARCHER SHOOTS US
DOWN, SO WE FALL AS WHOLESOME
RAINDROPS DESTINED FOR A
HIGHER GROUND?

I've fallen in love a million times, with you, I've seen through poet's lines on pages aged as autumnal leaves blown though a wish book of memories, opened when June blossoms tugged your mind on grandest brambles of humble kind, held wisdom words, encouragement, bold, to write of a passion in stories told through whispers bottled for ocean's keep, floating with flowers of devotion sweet as white roses suggest purity, youth, I've fallen in love with our truth.

*Y*ou nestled your mind inside mine for that while. Between daydreams, we discovered our treehouse. I decorated our door with lichens; they glowed (whenever our imaginations soared) to guide our way back home. Safety lived where we found each other. We peered through the veil draped at the window—viewed lifetimes we'd shared—spent our fleeting moments knowing each other so deeply (so deeply). Between daydreams in our playhouse, you slept on the loveseat. It gave me peace, nestled inside your mind for that while.

WHEN OUR STARLIT PATH DIVERGED,
I CLUTCHED MY WILL AND
DRAGGED HER INTO THE
UNKNOWN, ALONE.

FOR THE SELF

$\mathcal{I}$ stand alone and naked on the roadside while strangers rush by in cars blinded by busy lives and little time.

I wait for you to come.

Alone is taunting me. She wants me to spend my tears on your sometime sensibility, but she isn't frugal. I remind myself of this as I stand alone and naked on the roadside while strangers rush by. Alone soon realizes I've found my strength. She goes silent when a tear doesn't drop at my expense.

I wait for you to come.

Naked is whispering in my ear. She tells me I'm as unwanted as the dandelion standing next to me. I chuckle at the ignorance. The honey bee lusts for yellow blooms, so I draw strength from that flower. Neither unwanted nor unappealing, I stand tall and proud while busy lives rush by. Dandelion and I are nature's gems. Dandelion and I are wise.

We know you will not come.

I step out of Naked and leave her behind. Like a snake's skin, she lies on the roadside where you once would have met me on this solemn day.

I know you will not come and it doesn't matter to me.

I walk away from Alone. She keeps pace with my footsteps as a good shadow does, but I'll never welcome her inside. Not again.

I know you will not come, it doesn't matter to me, and I'm smiling.

I am no longer alone and naked while strangers rush by in cars blinded by busy lives and little time. No.

I'm with myself. I see me.

I'm dressed in myself. I feel me.

I no longer need your sometime sensibility.

Not today. Not tomorrow.

I'm free.

*D*oes knowing She diminish Me and all things wished for Me to be?

I trap Me between hope and disappointment in She's garden where daisies stretch necks to glimpse sunbeams penetrating nightsorrows—neither black, nor bright, atmosphere hovers thick, wanting. Hopes hurt where disappointment lurks in this space inside Me.

She watches. She waits.

I
claw earth
in search of comfort—
words to string onto my kite, bright
with bluebird yellows and raven reds—strong
and cheery as winter's sparrow nesting carefree
in a world delighted by a bird's bold.
High it flies where my kite begs
to try as I brush soil from my
blackened fingertips.
She watches. She
waits

.

I
tie
ATTITUDE
and
CONVICTION
to
TRUST
and
FAITH
to
ME

I fasten us to my kite while determination forces me to look She in the eyes.

She watches. She waits.

Does knowing She diminish Me and all things wished for me to be?

As it has before (and will again) buoyancy lifts me kiteward.

I laugh as Me flies from the garden inside—toward the future She grooms Me to see.

I would speak of the breeze, but rules whisper against such obvious observations in a March garden bed where blooms a love that is against the rules, too.

Beneath our tree, I ask leaves of grass if it hurts while they wait for their green to return.

The leaves look at me, silent.

Telling of a long winter is forbidden, too, so I pluck a blade of wanting-for-green and stroke it between my fingers while a wish for the chill to leave us takes flight toward a happier time of you and I and our in-between mind.

Sunshine I should not discuss peaks through clouds (that darken things I should not say) as if determined to set things right. It warms me as I contemplate not-green leaves in my shadow. We played here, you and I, during bedtime dreams long ago (on leaves of green under our canopy).

My shadow darkens as sunshine warms me, makes me smile, readies me for a new season (which is another topic forbidden), burns away clouds of a winter it's ridiculous not to mention because winter has a purpose, doesn't it?

The leaves smile at me. They know I know it does.

I tell them our love story (the story that rules say has no place in a poem because it's all been written before and nobody cares anymore). Nobody wants to read about

love,

hearts,

butterflies,

energizing springtime breezes joining sunshiny moments that warm me in a March garden bed.

The leaves giggle at me. They know I know my truth.

Beneath our tree, our sentinel waiting to bud in a March garden bed, I grasp my pen and paper and settle onto my fluffy quilt binding scraps of our remembrances—a blanket of comfort

—to write a love letter that will be delivered because it feels good to do so.

I may write of
butterflies,
hearts,
a season or three,
or an oceanic scene.
This poem is not for rules. It is for me.

Unlike leaves of grass beneath our oak tree in a March garden bed, I no longer hurt.

I own my green (no rules for me) and I choose to set it free.

This life I live is now my own.

        Past currents float my starlight soul toward a future ever calling me home.

I fear not end of my borrowed time.

Call it understanding.

Call it crazy.

Call it fulfillment.

This life I live is now my own

because I see in dreams of blue with you.

My heart leaps for chances locked safely away for this life—our destined truth.

I fear not painting magical hues.

Call me nature's child.

Call me brave.

Call me wild.

I see in dreams of blue with you

as our tomorrows gift us secret highs.

I'm to fly among eagles though my wings are broken and clouds blur my eyes.

I fear not soaring through obscure skies.

Call me brave.

Call me wild.

Call me nature's child.

Tomorrows gift us secret highs

because this life I live is now my own.

Free beyond senses locked in fire, earth, wind, and rain—I embrace my unknowns.

I fear not reaching beyond earth's rim.

Call it understanding.

Call it fulfillment.

Call it crazy.

This life I live is now my own.

ACKNOWLEDGMENTS

This book exists because a handful of loved ones and friends believed I should create it:

My husband. For over 25 years, he has encouraged and supported my artistic endeavors without fail.

My children. Their innocent wish to see Mom's book on a bookstore shelf pushed my passion to the next level.

Rainbow, who helped me persevere in the face of self-doubt.

My Ls, who encouraged this butterfly spread her wings.

My beta readers, who provided feedback that strengthened this chapbook.

So many poets, past and present, who continually inspire me to write better next time.

And finally, all the beautiful souls who have supported my poetry and prose on social media, particularly Instagram. Without your positive comments, encouragement, and excitement when I post something new, I wouldn't have had the drive to create this book. Always remember, your positivity makes a difference. It has for me, and it does for others. So, please, keep spreading those good vibes. The world needs them.

ABOUT THE AUTHOR

Ann Garcia has a Ph.D. in psychology. Her creative writing, which is highly introspective and emotion-driven, primarily explores nature, self, and love. She draws inspiration from waters and woodlands within the Great Lakes region of the USA and her life as a wife/artist/mother/scientist.

She is a contributor in publications by blood moon POETRY and Humana Obscura. She is active within the poetry community on Instagram where she's a member of The First Line Poets Project.

Find her on Instagram @solaceinraindrops and at www.riverblossoms.com.

instagram.com/solaceinraindrops

Made in the USA
Middletown, DE
21 June 2021